Chester Cathedral and City

Chester Cathedral

Described by K. M. Maltby
Canon Residentiary Emeritus of Chester

Hundreds of thousands of visitors come to Chester from all parts of the world every year. It is difficult to know exactly why they come but the evidence we have suggests that they come to see the Cathedral, walk round the walls, enjoy a stroll along the Rows, and in many cases go to see the notable zoo which is about three miles from the city centre. There is, of course, the River Dee too and this is probably the reason why people originally came to Chester. It is known, for example, that the Ancient Britons had a settlement in the area, and that the Romans called their settlement here 'Deva'. Indeed, we shall see much evidence of the Romans when we tour the city later.

It is the history of Chester's glorious Cathedral which we are concerned with here, however, and it is known that the present Cathedral probably stands on the same site as a much earlier church. In 1092 the first Norman Earl of Chester (a title still borne by the Prince of Wales today) brought a very able monk from Bec in Normandy to begin the building of a Benedictine monastery in honour of St Werburgh. This royal lady, daughter of the King of Mercia, died and had been buried originally in the Midlands. When the Danes advanced from the east in the ninth century her remains were brought to Chester for safe-keeping, most probably to the Saxon church standing on the same site as the one now occupied by the Cathedral. The monk who came from Bec was called Anselm, later to become Archbishop of Canterbury and a distinguished scholar of Christendom. The Abbey associated with him became a great pilgrimage centre in the Middle Ages as thousands of people came to worship at the shrine of St Werburgh there. Indeed, the Abbey Church of St Werburgh remained powerful for nearly five centuries until the Dissolution by Henry VIII, when, in 1541, it became the Cathedral Church for the King's newly-found diocese of Chester.

Thus Chester Cathedral as we know it was founded, and its varied history is fully illustrated by the various architectural styles seen in the masonry. The extension of the original Abbey buildings of 1092 was carried out by the monks and the military engineers (who were stationed at the castle in Chester), and building work in fact continued right through until the sixteenth century. Essentially the layout is fairly simple, although it may help to refer to the plan of the Cathedral opposite.

Front cover: The east front of Chester Cathedral
Back cover: The detached bell tower, designed by George Pace and opened in 1975

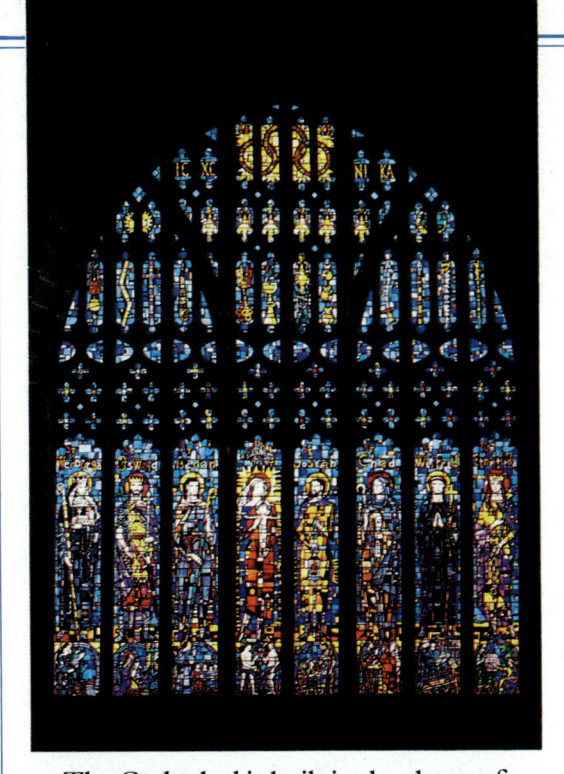

The Cathedral is built in the shape of a cross with the nave and quire running from west to east and the arms of the cross are formed by the transepts. By referring to the plan you will see that the south transept is much longer than the north, because the domestic buildings of the Abbey lie on the north side. The cloisters, dormitory, refectory, undercroft, the chapter house and its vestibule are all there. We are fortunate indeed that these monastic buildings are in a good state of preservation and they give us a very good idea of how the medieval abbey would have appeared.

It is difficult to stand back and enjoy a prospect of Chester Cathedral from the outside and in fact the best exterior view will be obtained when you walk along the city walls later. Most visitors find that the Cathedral is small enough inside to make it feel friendly and the local red sandstone with which it is built adds a certain warmth. A good starting place for a tour of the Cathedral is at the south transept door, then on to the nave, the quire, the lady chapel, the vestibule, the chapter house and after, on to the domestic buildings of the Abbey. If the weather is kind it is well worth spending a few quiet moments in the cloister garden.

In the abbot's passage in the undercroft at the south-west corner of the cloisters there is a regular audio-visual presentation which will help you make the most of your visit. At the north end of the cloister near the undercroft a bookshop sells a wide variety of goods.

It is difficult to pick out the most important features. The misericords in the quire are amongst the Cathedral's greatest treasures but contrastingly there is fine modern craftmanship to be seen in the nave quire stalls and in the great west window, which was constructed in 1961 and which depicts the Blessed Virgin, Holy Child, St Joseph and Northern saints. Other interesting features include the consistory court as well as the mosaics on the north wall of the nave. Pause too, to look at the lady chapel which dates back to the thirteenth century and which has three beautiful medieval ceiling bosses as well as the famous shrine of St Werburgh.

The chapels along the east wall of the south transept each have their own special interest, whilst up in the roof over the crossing there is again some fine modern work. By contrast, the oldest part of the Cathedral is the Norman arch in the north transept.

There is also much to enjoy in the monastic buildings, including the cloisters and the dormitory stairs. During the summer refreshments are available in the refectory which houses a unique pulpitum. Outside, the memorial gardens leading to the new bell tower are especially well-maintained, forming an attractive setting to the Cathedral buildings.

Opposite: An impressive view of the nave
Above: The west window

The crossing supports the square tower of the Cathedral with stout fourteenth-century pillars rising to 127 feet. The ceiling of the tower itself is supported by two fifteenth-century transverse arches which constitute a rare architectural feature which has been described as a 'crown-work of stone'. The ceiling of pitch-pine dates from 1819 and was made by two Chester joiners to the specification of Thomas Harrison, the Chester architect. In 1969 the ceiling was repaired and decorated in a red and gold pattern under the direction of George Pace. Modern lighting techniques were installed at the same time and it is now possible to see the ceiling properly from the floor of the crossing. Prior to 1969 it was virtually in permanent darkness. Up to this time the tower also housed the Cathedral bells but it was not strong enough to provide the support needed. In consequence, a free-standing bell tower (the first such in England since the Reformation) was designed and built adjacent to the city walls to the south-east of the Cathedral. This was opened in 1975. It is made of slate cladding on a sandstone base and contains an excellent ring of thirteen bells.

The quire starts under the eastern pillars of the crossing and is sectioned off from the aisles and the nave by fourteenth-century quire stalls. The quire is separated from the nave by a screen with a rood above it depicting a dramatic representation of the Crucifixion. This magnificent piece was carved in the Tyrol in 1913. The organ is situated to the north of the quire, having been moved there from the screen during the nineteenth century. Let into the floor behind the nave altar is a memorial to Dean Bennett who was Dean of Chester Cathedral between 1920 and 1937 and who 'opened' the Cathedral to welcome all visitors. The stalls in front of this are a fine example of the work of modern craftsmen and commemorate Dean Gibbs (1954-62).

Through the screen is the quire and the stalls – one of the great glories of the Cathedral.

Opposite: The ceiling of the central tower
Below: The quire screen

Overleaf, large picture: The quire
Small picture: Misericord depicting the legend of St Werburgh and the Geese

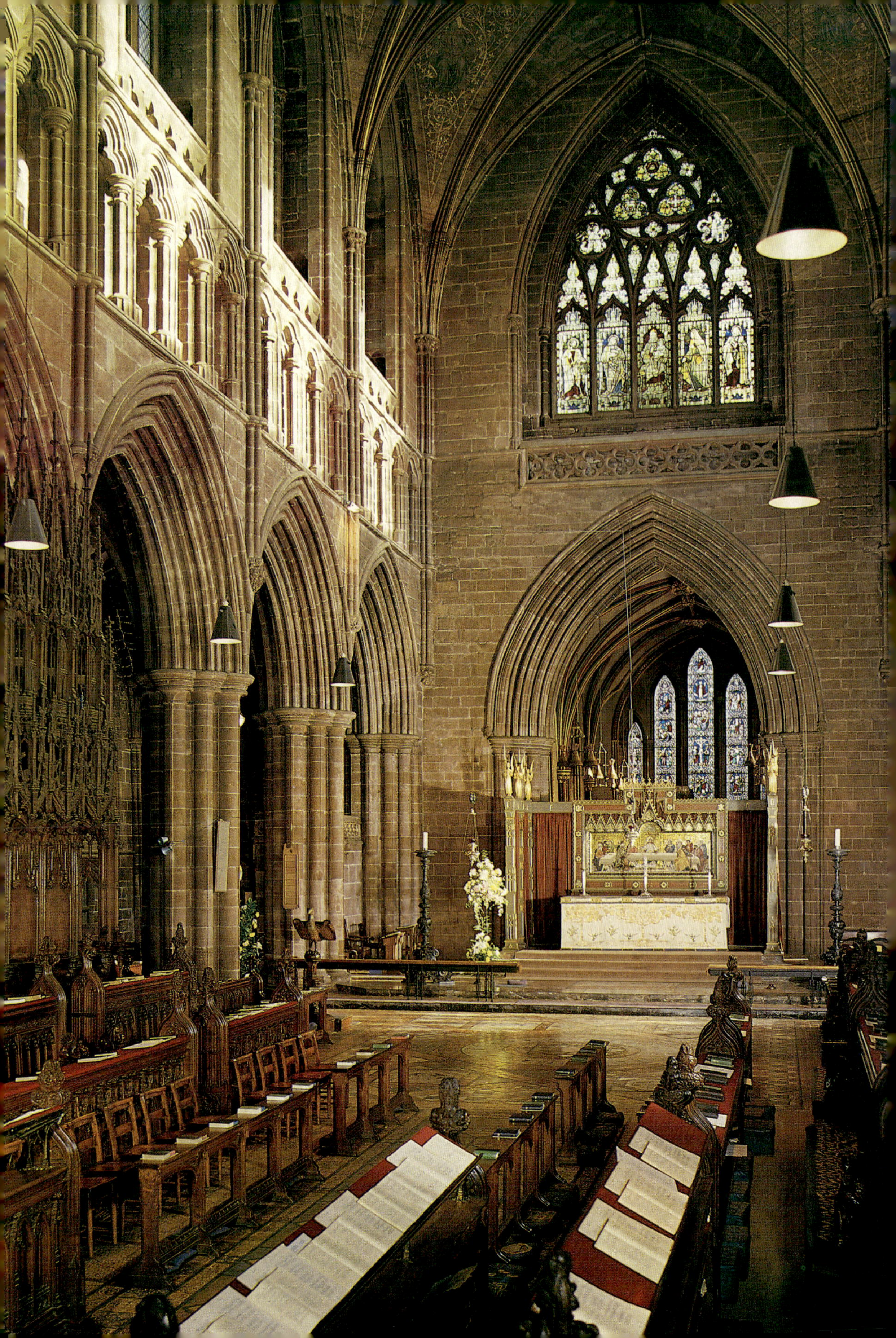

The quire was built in the thirteenth century, replacing one of Norman foundation. Later in the thirteenth century the enlargement of the Abbey was started by Simon de Whitchurch, together with the reconstruction of the entire east end of the building. The 700-year-old stonework in the quire is a beautiful example of the transition from the Early English to the Decorated style of architecture. In 1986 the Friends of the Cathedral sponsored the cleaning of the ceiling of the quire. This work, carried out by the Cathedral's own staff, brought to light a beautiful and colourful piece of nineteenth-century decorative work. In the ceiling panels of oak there are striking figures depicting Old Testament prophecy, angels and archangels. These rich and vibrant representations form a splendid tableau of faith and praise surrounding the centre of the Cathedral's worshipping life.

The magnificent canopied stalls deserve close attention, depicting as they do a whole variety of religious and mythical scenes. Each stall has a tabernacle which is a two-storey canopy, also elaborately carved, with tall wooden pinnacles rising from them. Even the arm-rests of the seats and the bench ends are beautifully carved.

The late F. H. Crossley wrote: 'Craftsmen and carpenters capable of designing and making such work were in good supply, and their ingenuity was apparently inexhaustible. The tall spires rising from a forest of pinnacles decorating the niches and canopies were the secret of medieval art unsurpassed since, and not thought of before.'

The misericords are also most interesting, being as old as the stalls with the same variety of rich carving. One tells the legend of St Werburgh and the Geese, one of the many legends attached to this saint. According to this one a flock of wild geese were ravaging the fields and the local inhabitants asked St Werburgh for help. A servant was sent to bring the geese but took one for a meal! The other birds flew around bewailing their loss. The bare bones were brought before St Werburgh and, in the words of Henry Bradshaw, a fifteenth-century monk of the Abbey, '. . . by the vertue of her benedyccyon the byrde was restored and flew away full soon.' The misericord (below) shows the bones on a dish, the bird flying away, while the servant confesses his guilt. The quire misericords are a useful reminder to us of the days when the Abbey flourished with its Benedictine rules of prayer, work and hospitality – traditions which are still to be found in the Cathedral today. Then, as now, the quire was the centre of the church's life of worship. Although the Abbey was prominent in the locality, it probably only had a company of about forty-five men in its heyday. Amongst the monks we remember are Simon de Whitchurch, Ranulph Higden, whose *Polychronicon* was written circa 1340 as an early attempt at recording history, and Henry Francis who is thought to have produced a script for the miracle plays which are still occasionally performed in Chester today.

There are many more curious figures to see in the carvings of the misericords, including a representation of Sir Gawain trapped in a portcullis and one of Tristan and Isolde beneath a tree in which her husband, King Mark, is hiding. Others include an elephant and castle, a monster killing a knight, a unicorn, wrestlers, Reynard the fox, Samson and the lion, an angel with a harp, and two herons, amongst many others.

The carvings on the bench-end of the Dean's stall are particularly noteworthy, depicting as they do the Tree of Jesse and ending with the coronation of the Blessed Virgin Mary. The Tree of Jesse has always been a familiar subject in Christian art and, in fact, there is another one carved on the opposite side of the quire, but the one on the Dean's stall is accompanied by a quaintly dressed pilgrim wearing a large hat and flowing collar.

Another interesting misericord carving is one of a man who seems to be drinking from a mug of ale as an imp tries to tip it towards him. This is not an old carving but there may be a personal reminiscence which lies behind it, as was sometimes found in church carvings.

The word Cathedral simply means 'a chair', and a Cathedral was a church in which the Bishop placed his chair - from which he could exercise his office as a teacher. With the passing of time the chair became known as the Bishop's throne and here it stands on the south side of the quire.

The high altar provides a stark contrast, having been enriched by the Friends of the Cathedral in 1957. Every generation must do what it can to enrich the House of God. The reredos is a mosaic by Antonio Salviati of *The Last Supper* and the whole ensemble is a most impressive piece of workmanship.

The high altar is the focal-point of Cathedral life; the praises of God rise daily in this place with music rendered in the tradition of English cathedrals.

It is from here that services are sometimes broadcast - a reminder of a great unseen congregation and perhaps to some a reminder of their visit to Chester.

Opposite, top: Misericord depicting elephant and castle
Opposite, bottom: The Dean's stall
Left: Misericord depicting man with jug of ale
Below: The high altar

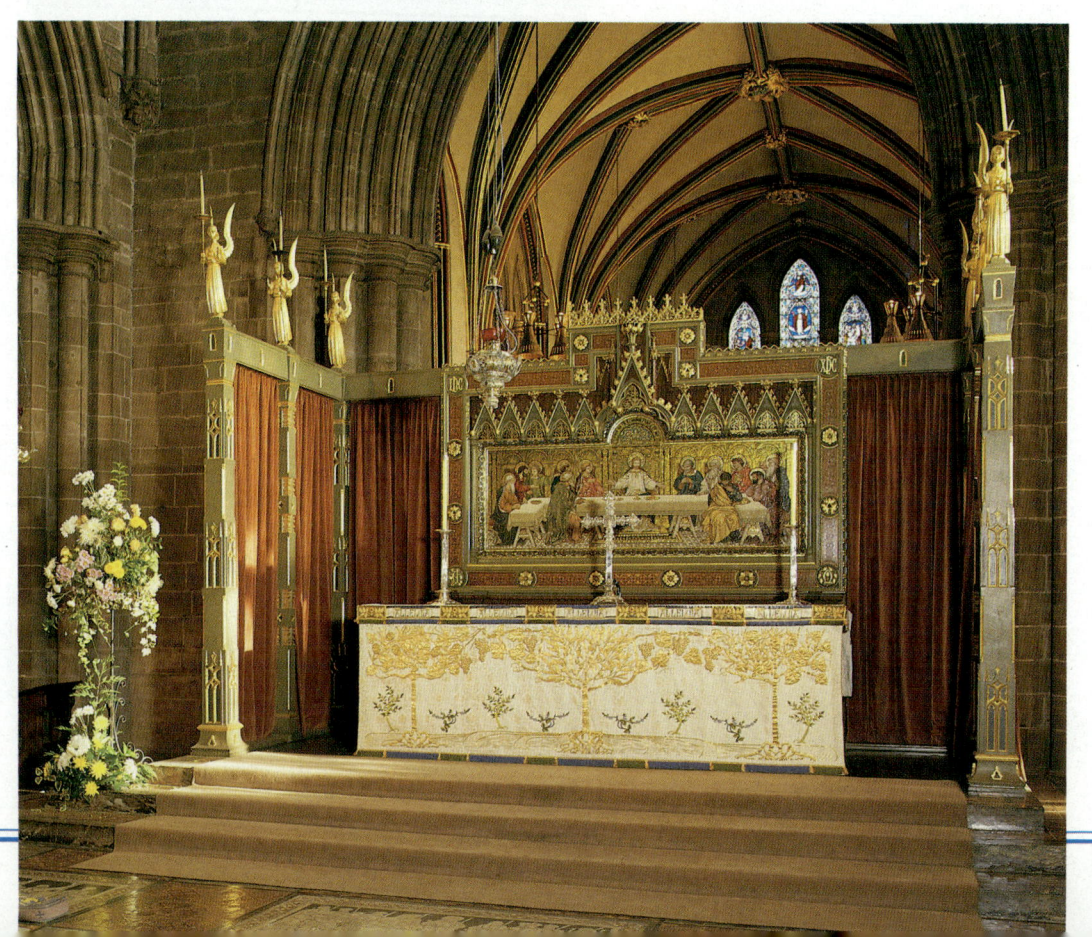

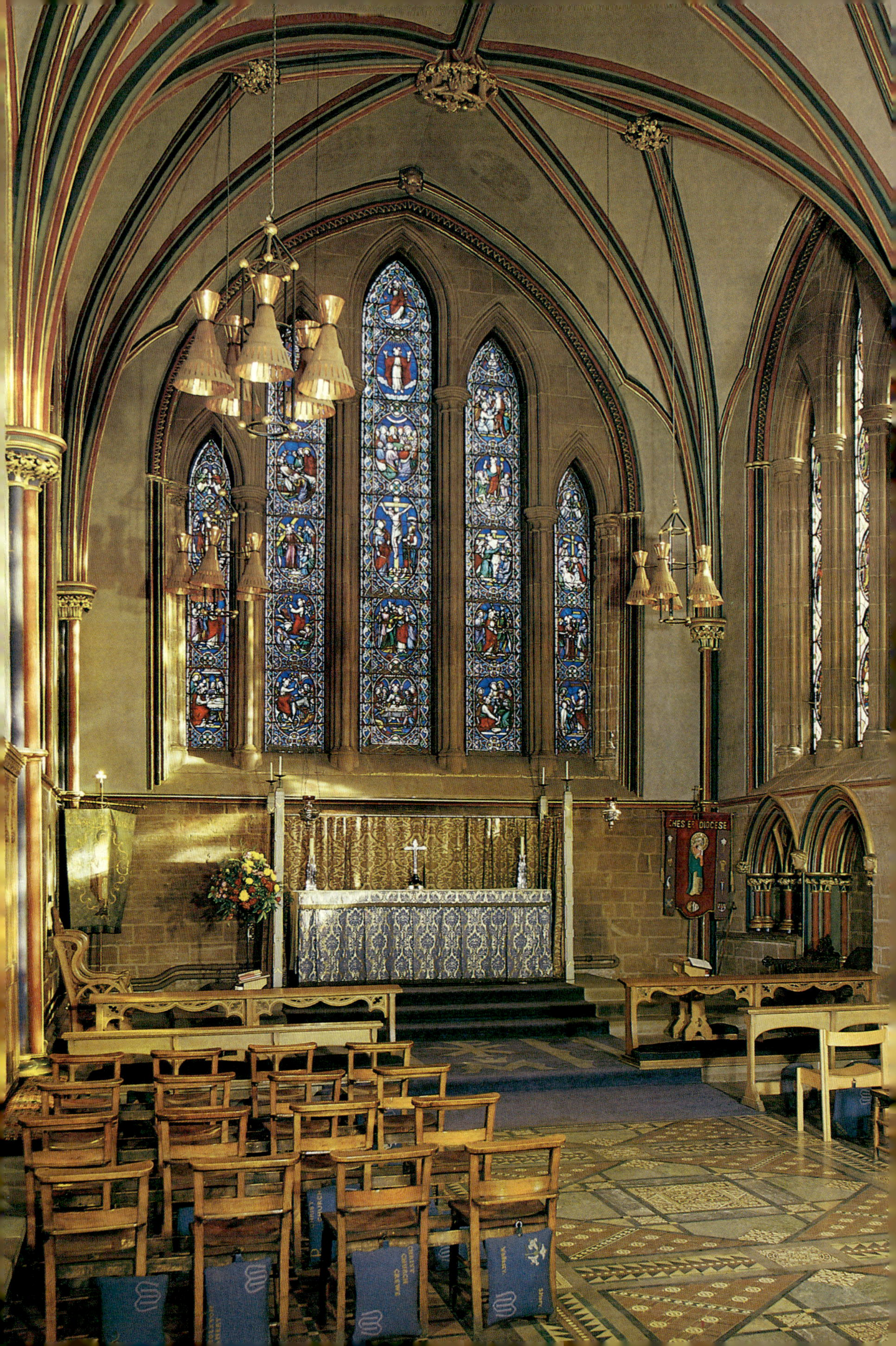
DIOCESE

The lady chapel is at the east end of the Cathedral and has been wonderfully restored so that it has a beauty all of its own. It is Early English in construction and probably dates from the time when Simon de Whitchurch was abbot between 1265-91, 'the greatest and most energetic of all the abbots of Chester'. This chapel then had fewer windows and the east one had only narrow lancets. Later, when the quire aisles were extended, entrances were cut into this chapel. Sad though it is to relate, there was a time in the sixteenth century when it was used as a consistory court and George Marsh was tried here for heresy and sent to the stake. Later the court was removed and then, in the nineteenth century, the south quire aisle was restored and shortened, so the entrance to the chapel on that side was closed. Further restoration went on and in 1859 and 1872 new windows were provided. Surviving all this there is the thirteenth-century vaulting and three richly-coloured bosses showing the Holy Trinity, the Madonna and Child and the matyrdom of St Thomas à Becket. St Thomas's girdle was amongst the relics kept by the monks here at one time.

At the west end of the lady chapel is the shrine of St Werburgh at which pilgrims knelt and made offerings to the Abbey. The shrine has been much restored but it once provided a canopy for the feretory containing St Werburgh's relics.

There are many other chapels regularly in use in the Cathedral today. The one in the south quire aisle is dedicated to St Erasmus, an early martyr who was a popular saint in the later Middle Ages, as well as the patron saint of seamen. On the left of the entrance of this chapel is the Battle Ensign of HMS *Broadsword*, Chester's ship. This chapel is set aside for private prayer and meditation.

Opposite: The lady chapel
Below left: The shrine of St Werburgh
Below right: Chapel dedicated to St Erasmus

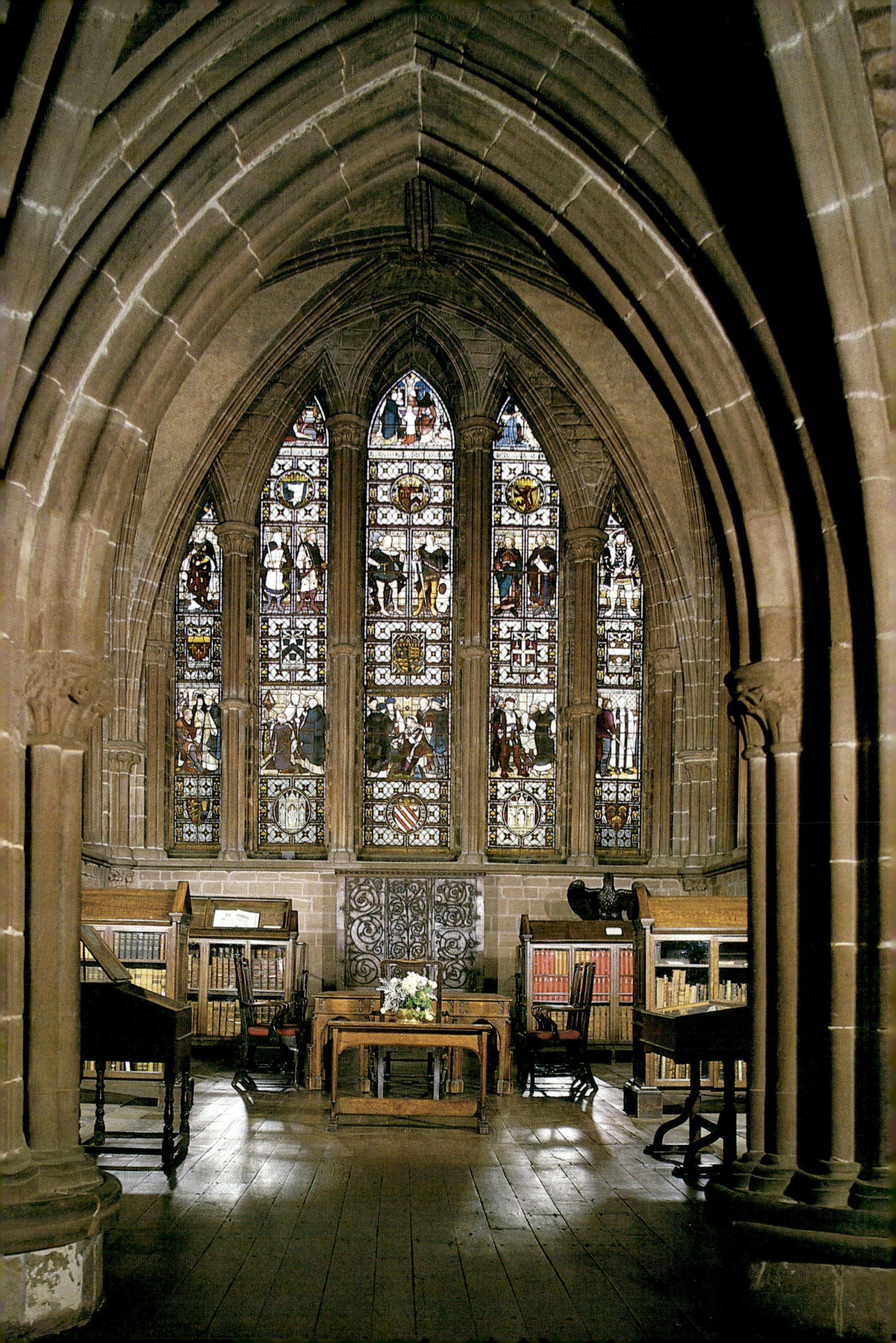

The chapter house, which is reached from the east cloister, was the place where the monks assembled to conduct their business and today the Cathedral Chapter, who are charged with the oversight of the buildings and their use, still hold monthly meetings there. The chapter house also contains part of the Cathedral library. It has a large vestibule with tall lancet windows, and in the east wall below a window there is a vast thirteenth-century cupboard overlaid with elaborate patterns of wrought iron. Amongst the manuscripts kept in the Cathedral are a beautiful copy of Higden's *Polychronicon*, a fifteenth-century Book of Hours, and a twelfth-century bible. Mention of these manuscripts reminds us that Cathedrals are still to be centres of learning, and a part of the Cathedral's library is to be seen in the chapter house. Visitors looking at the book stacks will see copies of works by great Christian writers (like St Augustine), or a set of the Rolls of England (which contains a translation of the *Polychronicon*), or again Calendars of State Papers. It is a very varied collection of books.

The cloisters themselves have been given stained glass windows which in sequence, anti-clockwise from the east cloister, trace out the calendar of saints throughout the year.

In the south cloister it is thought that the Abbots were laid to their rest, as you can see from the stones on display, and here also were carrells where the monks worked at their manuscripts.

From here the Cathedral can be re-entered via the north transept which has an impressive Norman arch and eleventh-century arcading. Adjacent to it is the tomb of John Pearson, Bishop of Chester between 1673-86 and a leading theologian of his time. His book on the Creed is a masterly exposition of Christian doctrine.

Opposite the north transept is the great south transept which was added to the Cathedral in the fourteenth century and which once formed the Parish Church of St Oswald.

Along the east wall of the south transept there are four chapels dedicated respectively to St Mary Magdalene, St Oswald, St George (the Regimental Chapel) and St Nicholas. Here Holy Communion is celebrated daily and we are again reminded that the Cathedral is not merely a museum, but a House of God where He is worshipped every day, for at the end, this is the reason for the Cathedral's existence.

The altar piece in St Oswald's chapel is the work of the woodcarvers of Oberammegau. Other features in the transept include a memorial to the first Duke of Westminster, a benefactor of both the Cathedral and city, the memorial book of the Cheshire Regiment, and a series of regimental flags, whilst on the west wall there is an interesting piece of machinery forming part of a carillon. As in most parts of the Cathedral, visitors will find descriptive labels to help them whilst looking round.

Opposite: The chapter house
Left: The north transept

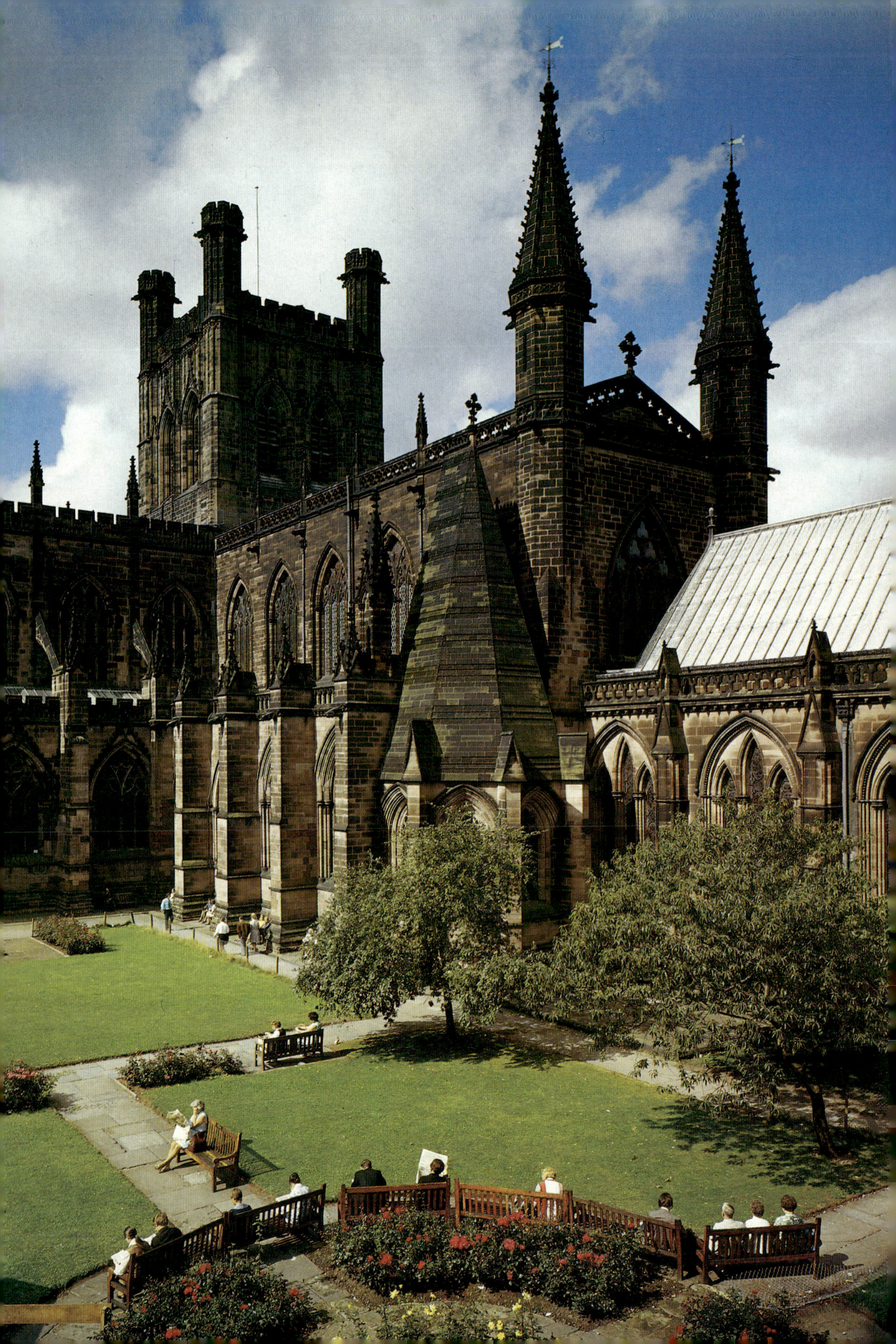

It is fitting that a visit to the Cathedral may come eventually to the refectory, a noble medieval room, where refreshments are served and one may sit for a time in splendid surroundings. This was where the Benedictine monks ate their meals and received their guests (who must have been many in the Middle Ages when Chester was a busy port).

When Henry VIII issued his statutes reconstituting the Abbey as a Cathedral he also founded a school, the King's School, and for a time, its scholars used the refectory. The school, though now sited in the Wrexham Road, still maintains close ties with the Cathedral.

A notable feature of the refectory is the beautiful stone pulpitum approached by an arcaded flight of steps from the south-east corner. From this a monk would read to his fellows when meals were taken in silence.

The refectory was re-roofed shortly before the outbreak of the Second World War and the handsome oak ceiling with its impressive beams dates from that time.

On the west wall of the refectory above the serving counter there is a large tapestry. It was commissioned by Charles I, woven at Mortlake and subsequently given to Bishop Bridgeman of Chester. A number of such tapestries were produced from a series of cartoons by Raphael for the Sistine Chapel in Rome. They depict incidents in the life and work of St Paul and this particular one is of the occasion recorded in Acts 13 when St Paul confronted the magician, Elymas.

As well as providing a place where visitors may refresh themselves, the refectory provides a setting for meetings and concerts, lectures, plays, and other social gatherings. It thus continues to be a centre of relaxation and fellowship very much in the pattern which has marked its function down through the years.

If time permits, a few moments spent in the cloister garth would enable this short tour of the Cathedral to end with a time of relaxation.

Opposite: The cloister garth
Below: The reader's pulpit in the refectory

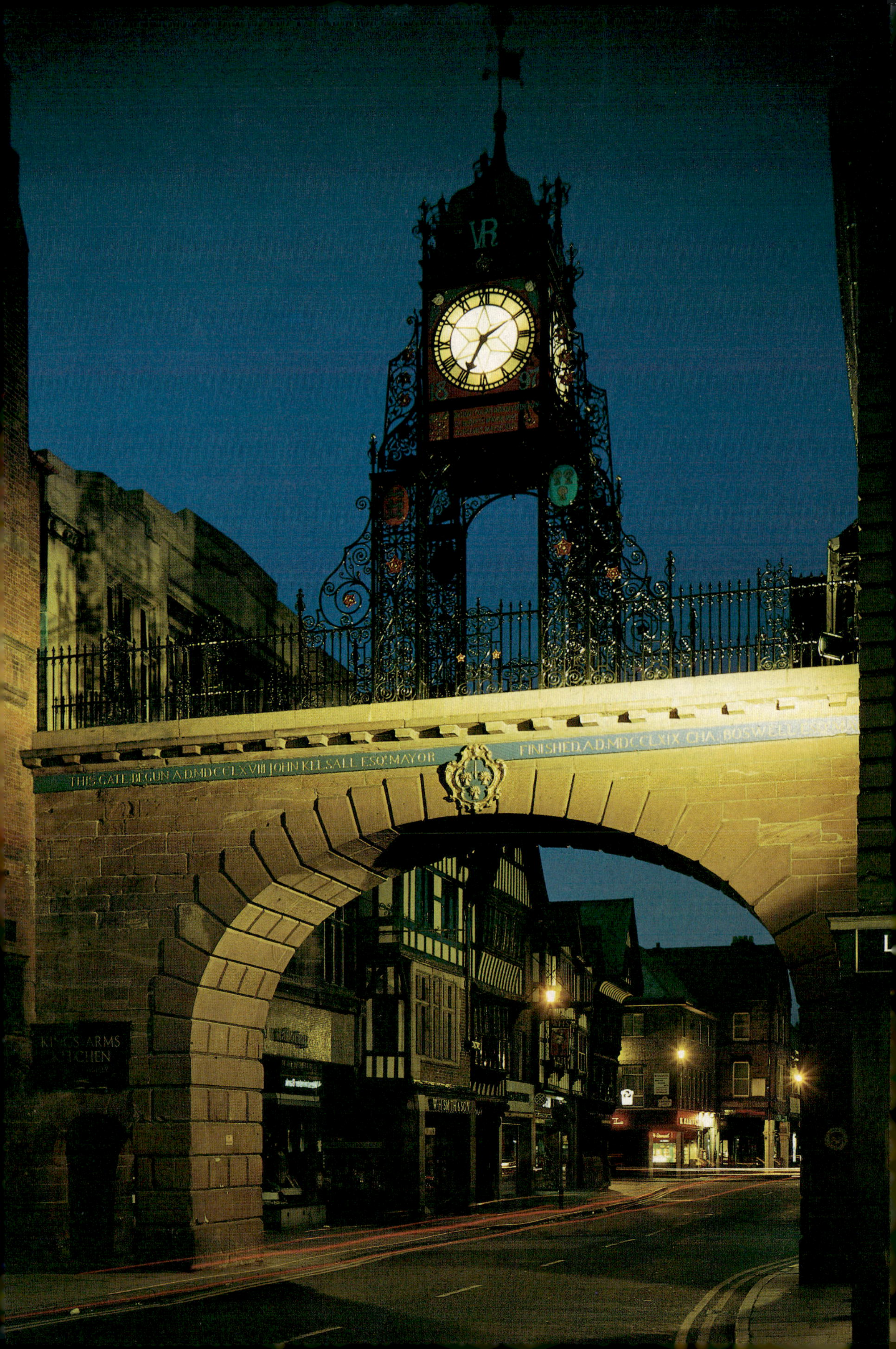

The City of Chester

The beautiful and historic city of Chester has much to offer visitors. Although now a thriving modern city, Chester retains a great deal of character and is unique in that it has been able to preserve a two-mile continuous circuit of town walls which give a fine prospect both over the city itself and out over the countryside beyond. The following pages are intended to give visitors a brief introduction to the main points of interest and have been arranged to form a substantial walking tour, starting from the Eastgate near the Cathedral.

The Eastgate is one of the many edifices in Chester whose history is inextricably entwined with the history of the city itself. Although the present Eastgate was built in 1768-9 at the expense of Richard, Lord Grosvenor, and the clock (probably the most photographed timepiece in the world after Big Ben) was erected in 1899 to commemorate Queen Victoria's Diamond Jubilee, it replaced a medieval gate which in turn had incorporated Roman arches. Tolls were originally charged on goods entering Chester at each of the gates in the city walls and traces of the eastern gateway of a Roman fortress were found during repairs to a nearby sewer in 1972.

This fortress had been built by the Romans at a suitable crossing point of the River Dee during the first century A.D. They called the fortress Deva and constructed many other buildings around it, thus forming the foundations of a settlement which was to become the future city of Chester. Roman remains abound in the area, and after passing the ruined fourteenth-century Wolf Tower a short distance south of the Eastgate, proceed still further south to the remains of a Roman amphitheatre situated opposite the Chester Visitor Centre in Vicars Lane which contains a life-size atmospheric reconstruction of a Rows street-scene circa the 1850s. The amphitheatre would have played an important part in Roman military life: the oval arena is thought to have measured 190 by 162 feet and there was accommodation for 7,000 people.

Opposite: The Eastgate and the Eastgate clock
Below: The remains of the Roman amphitheatre

Close to the Roman amphitheatre is the Newgate, a modern structure opened in 1938 and displaying the arms of the city as well as those of the Prince of Wales and the Grosvenor, Stanley and Egerton families. Just outside the Newgate is the peaceful Roman Garden which contains Roman remains found in the city including part of a Roman hypocaust or heating system.

Such remains serve to illustrate the enormous influence the Romans had on the Chester we see today even though they left the settlement here sometime in the fourth century A.D. Once they had departed there followed a period of 500 years - the Dark Ages - when little is known about Chester except that it fell into decay and it is thought that it was ravaged in turn by warring Britons, Scots, Northumbrians and Danes.

The picture becomes clearer during the ninth century when it is said that the body of the Saxon Saint Werburgh was brought to Chester from Staffordshire for protection against the Danes as mentioned earlier in this guide. At the beginning of the tenth century Chester was refortified by Aethelflaeda, Lady of the Mercians, daughter of Alfred the Great. She is believed to have restored the fortress, rebuilt and extended the walls and raised a castle on ground near the river, thus enabling the city to regain some of its former glory. One tradition also attributes the foundation of St John's Church just east of the amphitheatre to her. St John's Church was the Cathedral Church of the Diocese of Coventry between 1075 and 1102 and it became a parish church in the late 1540s. Part of the church fell into disuse and it now survives only as ruins. In 1881, the west tower collapsed and was never rebuilt, but the church's nave remains a superb example of Norman architecture. The church grounds adjoin the magnificent Grosvenor Park comprising twenty acres given to the city by Richard, 2nd Marquess of Westminster in 1867. This delightful area includes a scented garden for the blind and a statue of the 2nd Marquess by Thomas Thornycroft.

Having enjoyed a pause in Grosvenor Park there are several varied and interesting things to see in this south-eastern corner of the city. By returning to and ascending at the Newgate, the visitor can look west along Pepper Street which follows the line of the south wall of the Roman fortress westwards towards Bridge Street. It was originally the heart of St Michael's parish but its eighteenth and nineteenth-century houses were demolished in the late 1960s and Pepper Street was widened as part of the inner ring road scheme. Much of the north side is occupied by part of the Grosvenor-Laing Shopping Precinct which was opened in 1965.

By ascending the city walls at the Newgate, visitors can continue south along them to the Groves, where band concerts take place on summer Sunday afternoons and from where pleasure cruisers regularly depart. By descending from the walls at the 'Wishing Steps', which were constructed in 1785, and then the Recorder's Steps, you will reach this pleasant promenade. Delightfully tree-shaded, the Groves have an Edwardian bandstand, and are said to have associations with the Saxon King Harold. According to legend, he was not killed by an arrow that pierced his eye at the Battle of Hastings but came to Chester, where it is thought he lived as a one-eyed hermit in the Anchorite's Cell, a simple sandstone building to the north of the Groves.

Before descending the steps to the Groves, however, rest a while and pause to look down on the fascinating buildings in Park Street to the west, including the Albion public-house decorated with First World War memorabilia. Amongst the wide variety of black and white timber-framed houses you will see a row of six seventeenth-century houses which are confusingly known as the Nine Houses because they were originally nine in number! They have a timber-framed superstructure on a sandstone base which is a rare combination outside Chester. By the 1950s they had fallen into ruin but they were restored and improved during 1968/9.

Opposite: The Roman Garden
Below: The Nine Houses, Park Street

Adjoining this row of houses to the north is a large Victorian house which dates from 1881 and which bears the inscription 'The fear of the Lord is the fountain of life', an appropriate proverb for a dentists' surgery!

Further along, actually in Albion Street itself, there is the former Volunteer Drill Hall which was built for the Chester Rifle and Artillery Volunteer Corps, formed in 1859. Shaped like a miniature fort, the Drill Hall was opened ten years later.

You may decide to descend into this south-eastern corner of the city and explore some of the buildings more fully or you may proceed along the wall and then descend further along to join the Groves running alongside the River Dee. The pleasant southern riverbank is reached by means of an iron suspension bridge known as the Queen's Park Bridge because it links the city of Chester with the new suburb of Queen's Park. The bridge was first built in 1852 and it was rebuilt in 1923. A piece of the coiled steel used in its construction is preserved in a paperweight in the Town Hall.

The suburb of Queen's Park was laid out in the 1850s by Enoch Gerrard and many of Chester's more prosperous citizens moved to its desirable residences. The large neo-Georgian building erected in 1937 as the headquarters of the Army's Western Command dominates the south bank of the river although there are several other impressive buildings. A pathway along the south bank leads to the Meadows, which were formerly known as the Earl's Eye. These were a gift to the city by Mr and Mrs H. F. Brown in 1929 and were given on condition that they were always to be used for recreational purposes.

Nowhere in Chester is the delightful impact of the River Dee so evident than when strolling on the north bank and enjoying the splendid sight of the many boats which can always be found there. Indeed, regattas have been held on the Dee since the early nineteenth century. It is also possible to hire boats from various companies situated on the Groves and there are some cruises which sail past Eaton Estate, home of the Duke of Westminster.

Below: Queen's Park Bridge
Opposite: Half-timbered house in Park Street

THE·FEAR·OF·THE·LORD·IS·A·FOUNTAIN·OF·LIFE·

Walking westward from the Groves, the visitor will reach the Old Dee Bridge, a bridge whose varied history is fairly well documented. Until the nineteenth century the Dee Bridge was the only bridge at Chester and archaeological evidence found in Lower Bridge Street indicates that it may be on or near the site of a Roman bridge. Domesday Book describes arrangements for the repair of the bridge in the time of Edward the Confessor and other records show that it fell down again in 1227. It is also known that it was washed away in a flood in 1279 although a document of 1288 tells us that it was rebuilt by then in timber and stone. By the eighteenth century the Old Dee Bridge was considered 'very narrow and dangerous'. Today it connects Chester to the village of Handbridge, a traditional fishing community: the fishing industry still thrives on the river and fresh Dee salmon provides a delicious taste of Chester, along with the local Cheshire cheese.

The weir, to the north of the Old Dee Bridge, is said to have been built by Earl Hugh I in the eleventh century to provide water for the Dee Mills which had been owned by the earls of Chester and the Crown for hundreds of years, although they were purchased by the Wrench family in the eighteenth century. In the seventeenth century, eleven water wheels were in operation, and in 1913 the hydro-electric power station was opened on the site of the demolished mills.

Further west along the Dee, although not part of this tour, is Chester Castle, built by Hupus Lupus, a bloodthirsty Norman battlelord rewarded with the title 'Earl of Chester' by his uncle, William the Conqueror. Very little of the medieval castle remains and the current castle was actually rebuilt between 1788 and 1822. The nearby Grosvenor Museum is an exceptionally fine provincial museum housing an interesting section on the local history of Chester.

Below: The Old Dee Bridge and Weir

Above: Bridgegate

After admiring the bridge and weir proceed to the nearby Bridgegate which replaced a medieval gate built to guard the Old Dee Bridge. A tower was built above this medieval gate by John Tyrer in 1600, who used it to store water raised from the river. This water was then distributed through pipes to various properties in the city. The Bridgegate you see today was built in 1782.

If you continued along the city walls between the Bridgegate and the next bridge across the Dee in a westerly direction, you would come to the Grosvenor Bridge, although you would not be following the original line of the walls. This is because their route was altered slightly in the 1830s during extensions to Chester Castle. Grosvenor Bridge itself was designed by the architect Thomas Harrison who unfortunately did not live to see its completion. Its foundation stone was laid by Earl Grosvenor in 1827 after considerable pressure for improved communications between Chester and North Wales and it was the largest single-arch stone bridge in the world when it was opened and named by HRH Princess Victoria on 17 October 1832.

By proceeding along the walls past Grosvenor Bridge you would reach the Roodee, a feature unique to Chester, and once the site of the massive Roman harbour. Although now a famous racecourse, the Roodee took its name from the rood, or cross, whose base can still be seen there, and the word 'eye' which means land partly surrounded by water. The main meeting at Chester racecourse is held every May and its richest prize is the Chester Cup which started life as the Chester Tradesmen's Plate, first run in 1824. The foundation stone of the present grandstand at the racecourse was laid by the Duke of Westminster in 1899.

To visit all these places would obviously lengthen the tour considerably, so after pausing at the Bridgegate, you may prefer to descend and proceed into Lower Bridge Street, with its numerous historic and interesting buildings.

Lower Bridge Street leading into Bridge Street was a principal thoroughfare before Grosvenor Street was built in the 1820s and its many fine buildings give an indication of its former importance. The half-timbered Ye Olde King's Head, which was restored in 1934 and 1968, is just one example. It stands at the corner of Lower Bridge Street and Grosvenor Street and in the seventeenth and eighteenth centuries it was the home of the Randle Holmes of Chester. Four members of the family were antiquarians and herald painters and Randle Holme II made the first attempt at organising the city archives.

Further along is St Michael's Church which now houses the Chester Heritage Centre, Britain's first architectural heritage centre, which was opened in 1975. St Michael's was one of the city's smaller parish churches, first mentioned in a charter issued by Henry II *c.* 1154. As a heritage centre it now encompasses all aspects of the city's heritage with a programme of exhibitions on historic, archaeological and architectural themes.

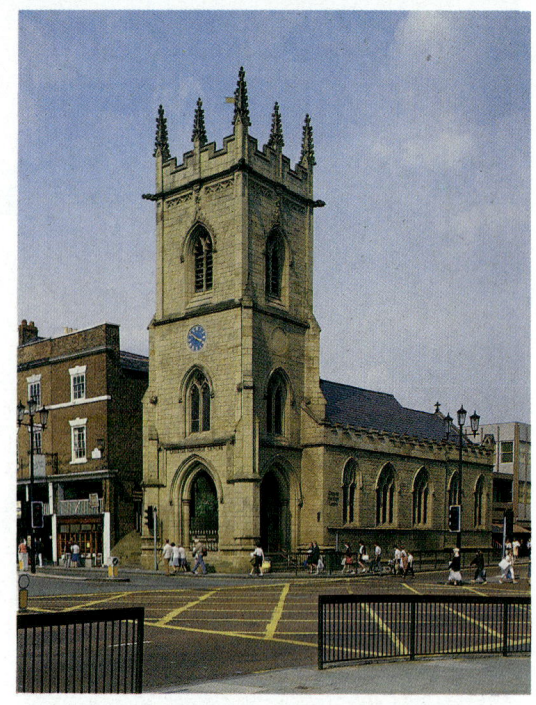

Above: Chester Heritage Centre (formerly St Michael's Church)
Below: Ye Old King's Head, Lower Bridge Street

Above: The Bear and Billet Inn, Lower Bridge Street
Below: The Falcon Café, Lower Bridge Street

Lower Bridge Street also has several other buildings before the heritage centre worthy of mention. Just inside the Bridgegate is the Bear and Billet, a black and white tiered building which dates from 1664 and which was once a town house of the earls of Shrewsbury. The Three Kings Studio adjoins the Bear and Billet to the north, and like the nearby Gamul House and Terrace, this building has an eighteenth-century façade. Gamul Place at the rear is a superb example of Chester's conservation programme with nineteenth-century terraced cottages being successfully restored and modernised.

The Falcon at the corner of Lower Bridge Street and Grosvenor Street was re-opened as an inn in 1982, also following a major programme of restoration. It is a seventeenth-century timber-framed building which was once the town house of the Grosvenor family.

Pause also to look at Bridge Place, St Olave's Church, the Albion Hotel and the Tudor House.

Top left: All-weather shopping in the Rows
Top right: Chester Town Crier
Bottom left: The Rows, Bridge Street
Bottom right: God's Providence House, Watergate Street

There were once Rows in Lower Bridge Street and a few traces still survive there, but by proceeding on to Bridge Street, Eastgate Street and Watergate Street, you will be able to see them in their fully developed form. The Rows are Chester's world-famous feature and consist of galleries of shops above the stores at street level, reached by steps from the main thoroughfares, enabling visitors to do their shopping in perfect comfort, sheltered from the elements.

The origin of the Rows has never been fully explained. Some believe they were built as a town planning exercise after a fire in 1278 which destroyed most of Chester. Documentary evidence suggests a gradual development, however, which lasted from the thirteenth to the eighteenth century. It is known that by the middle of the fourteenth century there were both stalls at street level and the Rows themselves. Documentary evidence of the sixteenth and seventeenth centuries indicates that buildings were erected which overhung the Rows and the streets, posts being erected to support the overhang. Finally the vacant space created by the posts at street level was filled in.

Apart from the Rows, Bridge Street has a number of other interesting features. Owen Owen's department store, for example, incorporates three medieval arches at Row level and the building is consequently known as the 'Three Old Arches'. The 'Dutch Houses', so called because they are said to resemble a Dutch style of architecture, date from the seventeenth century and contain a fine seventeenth-century plaster ceiling. The houses can be recognised by their twisted pillars. Number 12 Bridge Street now houses a bookshop but incorporates a medieval crypt which is thought to date from about 1270-80. You can also visit the delightful Toy Museum in Bridge Street which contains an extensive collection of playthings through the ages and the largest display of Lesney/Matchbox products in the world.

Number 55 Bridge Street is an ornate Victorian black and white building decorated with a statue of Charles I, and further north, number 47 dates from the seventeenth century and used to be used as St Michael's Rectory. The most impressive building on that side of the street, however, is probably the massive entrance to St Michael's Arcade. This was built in 1910 in the Baroque style and there was a public outcry when the 2nd Duke of Westminster who owned the site ordered it to be demolished and replaced by the present black and white structure.

At the junction of Bridge Street, Northgate Street, Eastgate Street and Watergate Street, you will see the Cross, which has been so important throughout Chester's history. A High Cross where merchants struck bargains stood on this site from 1407 until the English Civil War, and after a short period in the Roman Garden, it was re-erected in the centre of the city in 1975. For many centuries the Cross was the centre of city government. Nowadays, a town crier stands at the Cross and issues proclamations to passers by daily at 12 noon and 3pm from Tuesdays to Saturdays between April and September.

St Peter's Church at the Cross is probably of Anglo-Saxon origin but the rest of the buildings in the vicinity are mostly Victorian, the ornate half-timbered building on the corner of Bridge Street and Eastgate Street dating from 1888.

From the Cross, there are obviously several routes you can take and you may even choose to end the tour here and return to the Cathedral via Northgate Street or Eastgate Street. If you decide the latter, spare a few minutes and firstly proceed westward along Watergate Street. There, on the south side of the street, you will see a most unusual building - God's Providence House. The date 1652 and the inscription are thought to celebrate the fact that the house's occupants were spared from the plague. There were plans to demolish God's Providence House in the 1860s but the Chester Archaeological Society protested and the house's

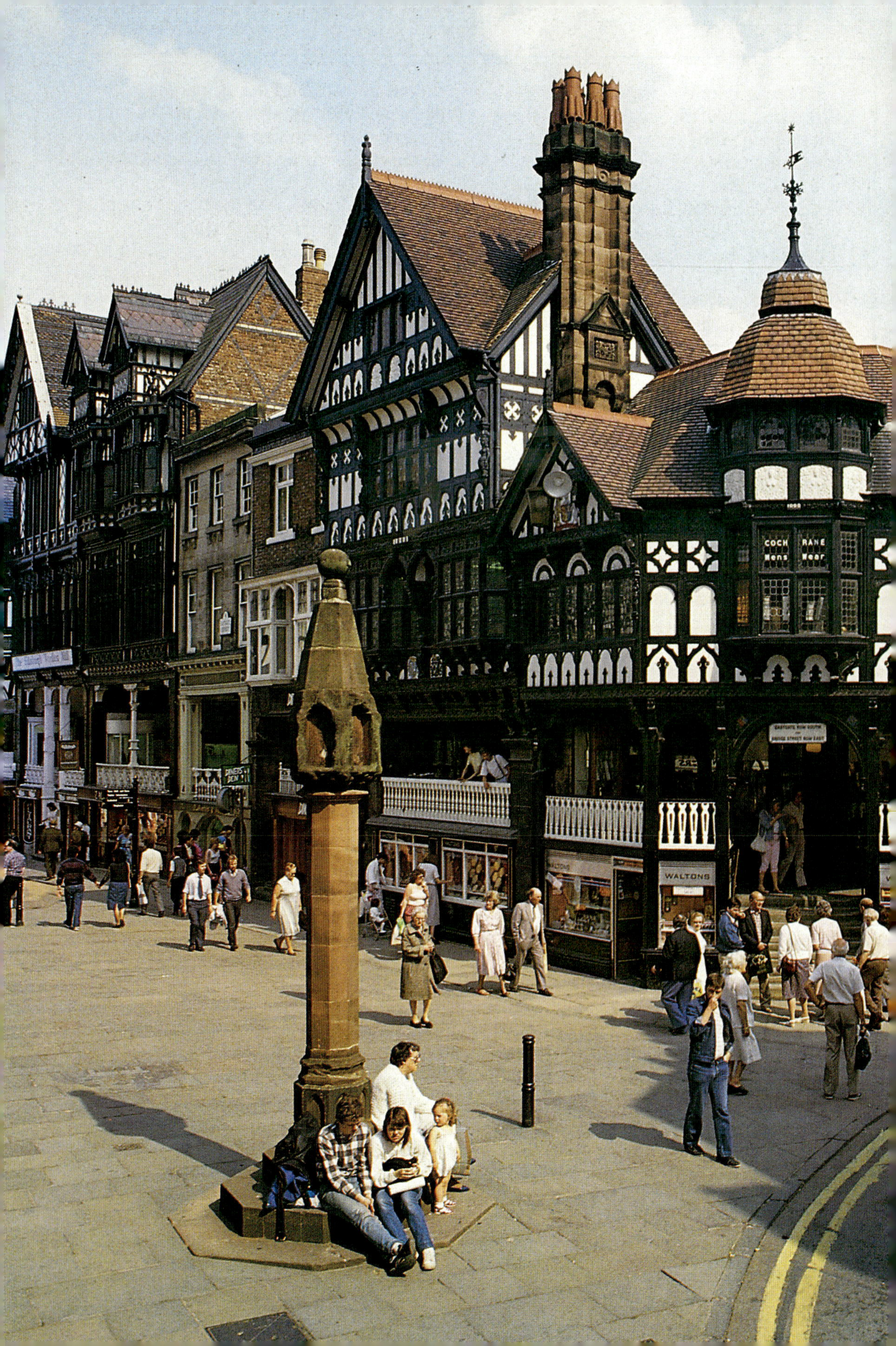
COCH RANE
Mens Wear
WALTONS

reconstruction was supervised by James Harrison.

You may prefer to head northwards on Northgate Street. This way you can also take in the Town Hall without making too much of a detour. Chester Town Hall in the Market Square was built between 1865 and 1869, being opened by HRH The Prince of Wales on 15 October 1869. It replaced a late seventeenth-century Town Hall known as the Exchange which was destroyed by fire in 1862. The current Town Hall was designed by the architect William Henry Lynn of Belfast and was built in the Gothic style.

From the Town Hall you will be able to see the starting-point of the tour at the Cathedral. Guided walking tours escorted by Blue Badge City Guides leave the Tourist Information Centre at the Town Hall at 10.45 a.m. daily (except Sundays) all year round including Christmas Day!

It is interesting to note that both the Cathedral and the Cross are now occasionally the scenes for revived performances of Chester's mystery plays, religious plays which used to be of some importance to the life of the city. They were also known as the Whitsun plays as they took place during three days of Whitsun week. It seems likely that they originated as an attempt to make the Latin teaching of the Church more intelligible to the general public, and although many cities are known to have had them, Chester's are considered to be the oldest, dating from about 1375.

If you still have stamina left once you have reached the Cross, however, continue the tour by taking a slow walk down Watergate Street, which since 1966 has been divided by the inner ring road, but which once led to the old harbour. Ships used to tie up by the Watergate at the foot of Watergate Street until the fifteenth century, but at about that time, the estuary began to silt up and boats were then forced to anchor about twelve miles downstream. Despite efforts to create new havens nearer Chester, the trade of the port declined.

Next to God's Providence House, mentioned earlier, there is a wine bar whose premises incorporate the largest medieval crypt in Chester, probably dating from the thirteenth century.

Nearby is the Leche House which is named after the Leche family of Carden and which has associations with Catherine of Aragon. Pomegranates, which were the symbol of Aragon, are represented in its ornate plasterwork, and there is also a gallery with a squint hole concealed by a grille.

Continuing westwards, one of the next buildings worthy of note is Bishop Lloyd's House which was restored by Chester City Council in 1973-76. It is named after George Lloyd, Bishop of Chester between 1605 and 1615, whose daughter Anne married Thomas Yale, after whose grandson Yale University in the United States of America is named. The house is a richly carved building, including several carvings of biblical scenes and heraldic beasts. Some think that it is the richest example of carved timberwork in the city, and despite being restored, it retains an impressive appearance of age. Inside there is some splendid panelling.

The north side of Watergate Street is dominated by the Georgian elegance of Booth Mansion, a fashionable Assembly Room in the eighteenth century, but now home to the Chester branch of Sothebys. The Row at Booth Mansion is supported by stone arches, probably of the fourteenth century, and beneath is another of Chester's medieval vaulted cellars. Further along on the north side, Nos. 38-42 Watergate Street, behind modern façades, contain substantial remains of a large medieval house.

Trinity Church, another medieval church, stands on the corner of Watergate Street and the inner ring road, but it was declared redundant as a church in 1961. It is now the Guildhall of the Freemen and Guilds of the City of Chester and twenty-three companies are represented. The Custom House of the Port of Chester, dating from 1869, is also here.

Opposite: The Rows at the Cross

Once beyond the inner ring road, Watergate Street slopes sharply to the Watergate. Stanley Palace, an ancient building, is situated on the southern side of the street. It is said to have been built by Peter Warburton in 1591 and to have passed to the Stanley family of Alderley in the seventeenth century. The Earl of Derby acquired it in 1899 and assigned it on a long lease to Chester City Council in 1928. The Council completely restored it in the 1930s when the right-hand gable and frontage were also added. The restoration work has been carried out very successfully.

Watergate House, situated to its west, is a large classical brick building which was built by Thomas Harrison in 1820 for Henry Potts, Clerk of the Peace for Cheshire. It has an unusual circular hall and the entrance is set at an angle.

The Queen's School was housed at 104 Watergate Flags from 1878 to 1883 before it moved a little further north. Number 104 now contains a rare sedan chair porch with a door on two sides which was restored in 1981. The Queen's School, however, was founded with the support of the 1st Duke of Westminster to educate the daughters of the middle classes and the Duke obtained Queen Victoria's permission for its name in 1882. The school now occupies the site of the city gaol which was opened in 1808 and closed in 1972. This would have been a large rectangular building with a western entrance facing the city walls so that the public could watch the executions.

The Royal Infirmary adjoins the current Queen's School to the north 'in a situation peculiarly healthy, being removed from the noise of the streets, and open to the fine air from the estuary of the Dee and the Welsh mountains'. It was founded in 1755 and opened in 1761, being built upon one of the Roman cemeteries of the city. Dozens of burials have been discovered in the area as well as other items such as lamps, trinkets and coins.

The actual Watergate itself was built in 1788 and, before it silted up, the River Dee ran close by. The Watergate faces the

Roodee and Chester Racecourse, as described earlier, and this whole area was in medieval times covered with water. Indeed at the back of the county grandstand at the racecourse there is a stretch of wall, forty feet in front of the medieval city wall, which is thought to be part of the Roman quay. Several Roman burials have also been found close to the walls here. By ascending the city walls near the Watergate the visitor can enjoy the remainder of the tour by strolling along these vast walls, taking in the varied scenes both within and without them.

The walls now vary between fifteen and twenty-five feet high and average between five and six feet in width. The wall-walk was probably originally defended to the outside by crenellations, since replaced by triangular coping, so that much of the wall above the walkway is not original. In many places, the walls are medieval over Roman foundations, and it seems difficult to believe that the earliest walls consisted only of turf ramparts surrounded by wooden palisading overlooking a ditch on the outside. Parts of this Roman wall can still be seen between King Charles' Tower and the Northgate. The medieval work was carried out in the local brown sandstone for extra protection during the Civil War. The damage inflicted then was repaired in the time of Queen Anne with little attempt being made to preserve the medieval details.

During the eighteenth century the value of the walls as a pleasant city promenade was recognised and the medieval gates were replaced by new gates in the form of bridges to preserve the walkway.

The maintenance of the walls has always been of importance, so much so that in the past officals were appointed to collect special taxes for their upkeep.

By strolling northwards you will reach the north-west angle of the walls. In this corner the rectangular Bonewaldesthorne's Tower acts as a defended entrance to the

Opposite: Stanley Palace, Watergate Street
Above: The Watergate

spur wall leading to the water tower, originally built between 1322 and 1326 to defend the former habour. A detailed contract of the time reveals that the architect of the water tower, John de Helpeston, was paid just £100 to construct it. Nearby is the canal basin and tower wharf, where horse-drawn canal barge cruises depart frequently throughout the summer. There is an excellent view of the canal and railway from the water tower and there is a staircase of three locks lowering to the Chester Canal.

Continuing east along the walls will take the visitor across the Northgate, the fourteenth-century version of which contained a prison. The Northgate you see today was designed by Thomas Harrison in 1808 and is a typically classical arch.

There is a good view of the historic Bluecoat School from this section of the walls. The school was built in 1717 to house a charity school which had been founded in 1700 by Bishop Nicholas Stratford. The school closed in 1949.

Continue eastwards to reach the tower which was first known as Newton's Tower, then the Phoenix Tower, and which rises some seventy feet above the Shropshire Union Canal running alongside it.

It latterly became known as King Charles's Tower because Charles I stood on it on 24 September 1645 and witnessed the defeat of his army at Rowton Moor east of the city. The following day the King rode over a bridge across the Dee and off into Wales, but Chester itself then faced a crushing two-year siege and only plague and wartime rations of cats and dogs forced the citizens to surrender. Much of the city had by then almost been destroyed, a fact which makes it all the more remarkable that Chester has managed to preserve so much that makes it such a delightful place to visit today.

A short walk southwards along the walls will take you back to the vicinity of the Cathedral from whence the tour began.

The selection of places included in this guide can only be a brief sample of the marvellous attractions Chester has to offer, and it is well worth staying longer to discover this historic place in more detail.

Below left: The Water Tower
Below right: King Charles' Tower